KISSING ZONE

Volume Two

NYC

by

Darling J. Miramey

Cover Arts
Kissing Zone II 24
by Darling James Miramey
medium: acrylic on canvas,
dimensions: 60 x 48 in (1524 x 1219 mm)

www.miramey.com
office@miramey.com

This work is fiction. Names, characters, and incidents either are the product of the author's imagination or are used fictitiously. Any resemblance to actual persons, living or dead, events, or locales is entirely coincidental.

Books may be purchased in quantity and/or special sales by contacting the author.

FIRST EDITION February 14, 2025
Miramey, New York, NY
Printed in the United States of America
*
ISBN 979-8-9925730-0-8

Midtown Mirage

Midtown's heart, dreams take flight,
Wet lips met under neon light.
A kisses, like Broadway's glow,
City endless, hooked show.

Subway Flow
Chinatown crowded, swinging car,
Oriental tempt, hearts afar,
A brush of lips, a spark took beat,
New York's steamy underground's heat.

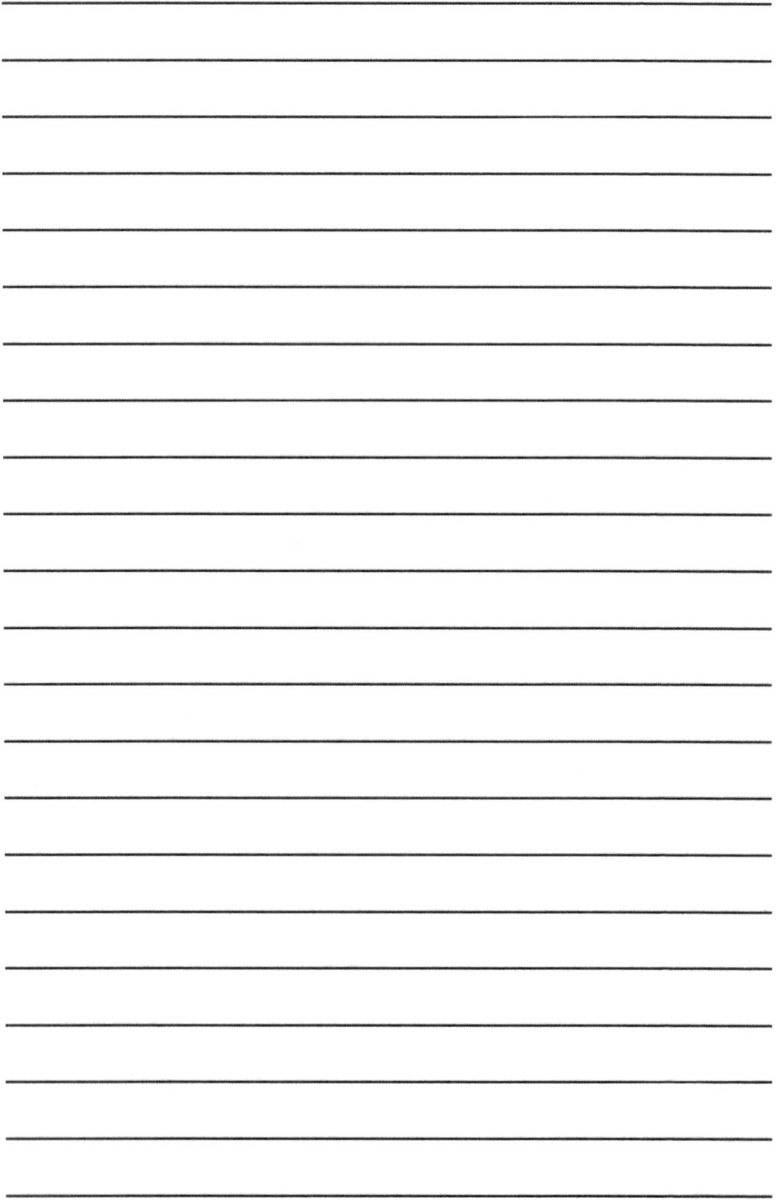

Central Park Chance
A stroll through Park's green land heart,
Led to a kiss, set us apart,
Under willow branches swaying,
Blossoms unexpected staying.

Brooklyn Bridge Whisper
Suspension cables above crake,
Entwined, a close-up we take
As dusk painted the city's glow,
Lips met softly, hearts beating grow.

_____

_____

_____

_____

_____

_____

_____

_____

_____

_____

_____

_____

_____

_____

_____

_____

Times Square Temptation
Neon lights kaleidoscope haze,
Lips paraded, crush city's daze,
Amidst the kiss square, we are found,
A moment's of peace, where resounds.

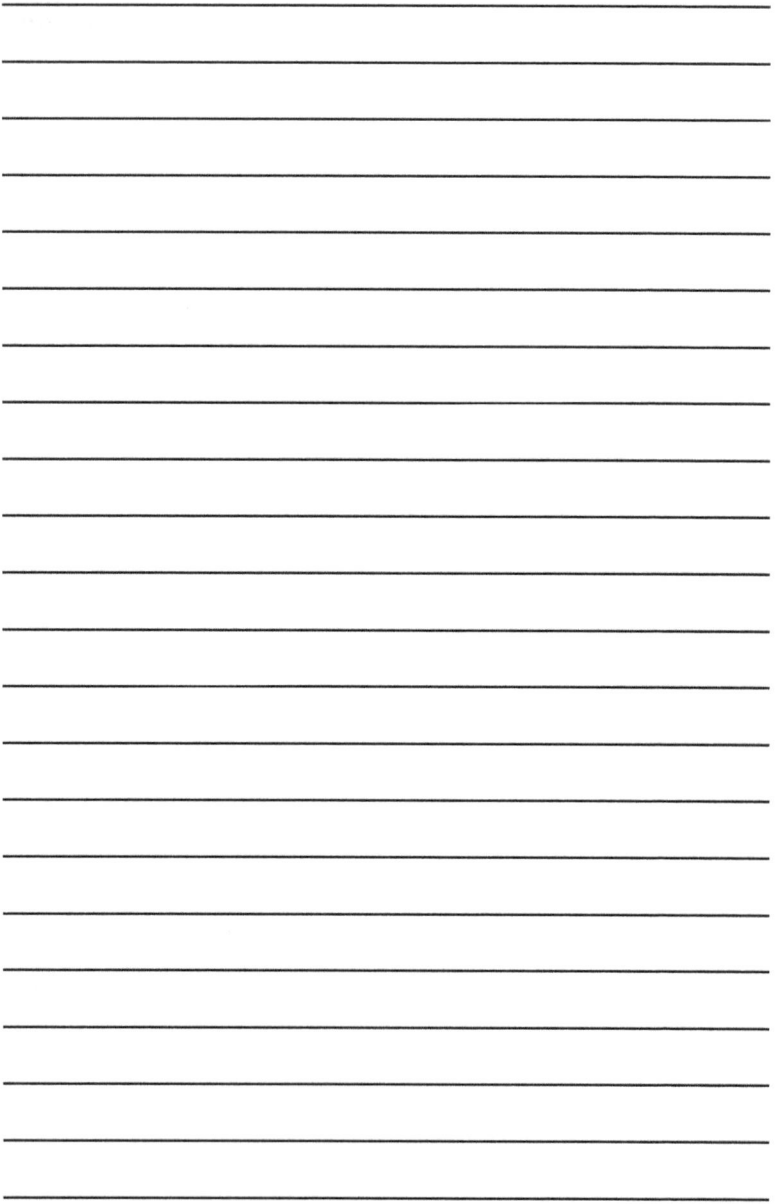

Greenwich Village

The quaint shimmer of Village lamps,
You shone bright, extasy dance,
Lips met softly, sealing sweet bond,
Greenwich's highly romantic pond.

_____

_____

_____

_____

_____

_____

_____

_____

_____

_____

_____

_____

_____

_____

_____

_____

_____

Coffee Shop Crush
Cozy, Upper West Side café,
Steaming cups, lips, our hearts swayed,
Gentle kiss flavored coffee's zest,
Way to desired sensual nest.

Pizza Parlor Passion
Little Italy's warm embrace,
Flavors scent, intertwined space,
Slice of heaven, kissing so fine,
A delicious crisp dream of mine.

_____

_____

_____

_____

_____

_____

_____

_____

_____

_____

_____

_____

_____

_____

_____

_____

_____

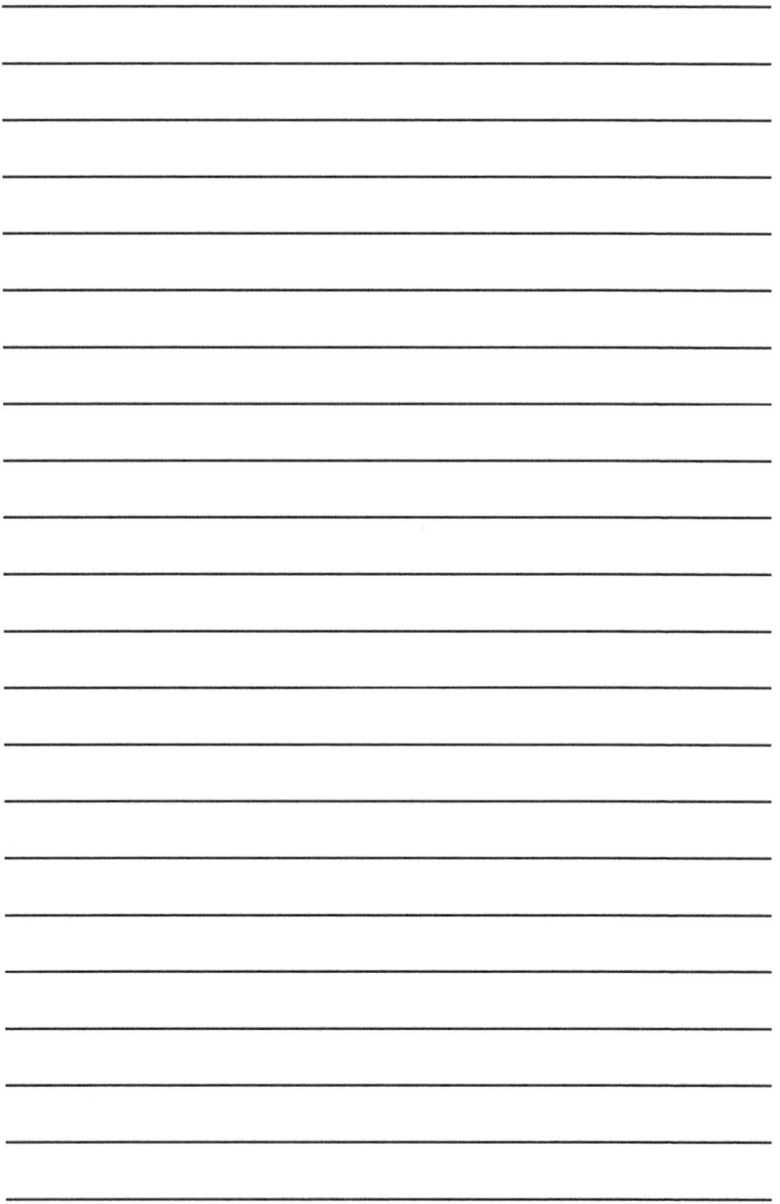

Winter Bagel Bliss
Cream cheese kiss, a perfect blend,
Hot coffee's tongue, seductive friend,
Carpet, couch and desk set the stage,
Together on Valentine page.

_____

_____

_____

_____

_____

_____

_____

_____

_____

_____

_____

_____

_____

_____

_____

_____

_____

Wine and Cheese Whispers
SoHo bar, kisses very low,
Each lips exotic touching flow,
Modern twist sensual affair,
Coming soon... now, wine and cheese pair.

_____

_____

_____

_____

_____

_____

_____

_____

_____

_____

_____

_____

_____

_____

_____

_____

_____

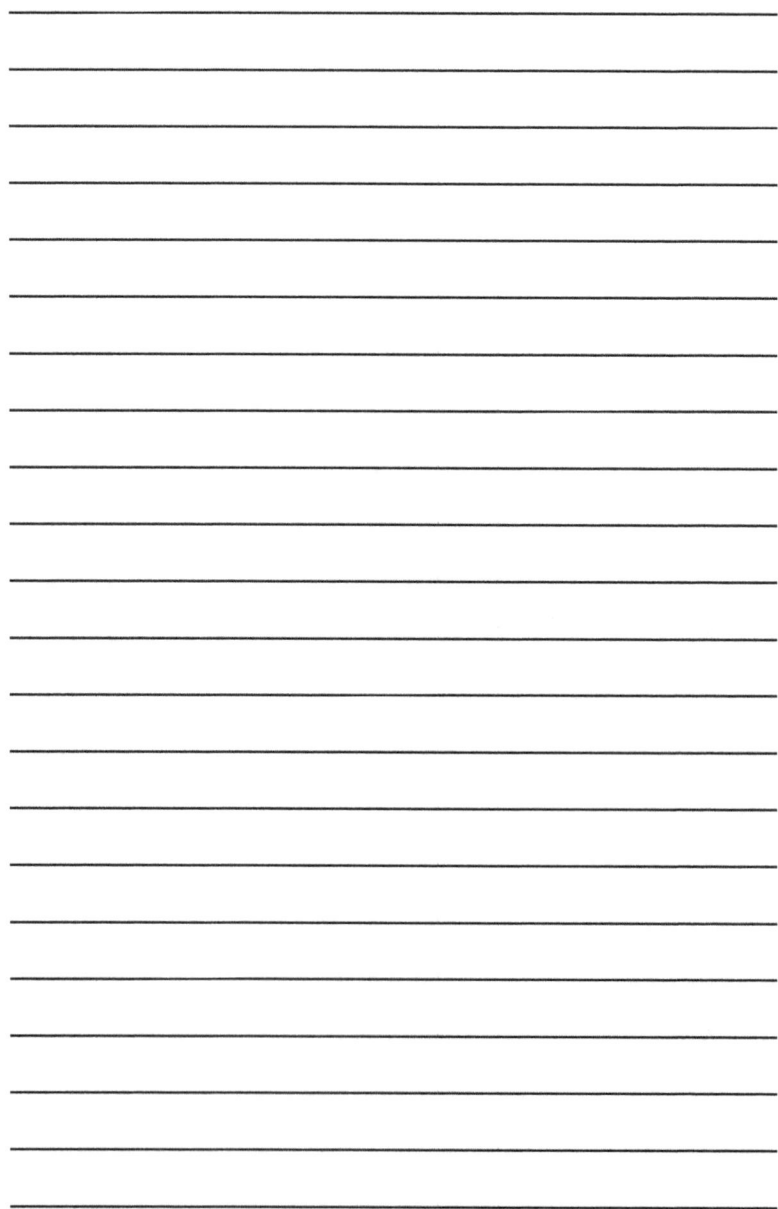

Dessert Seduction
East Village chic patisserie,
Sweet treats tempted, appetite spree,
A tender kiss mid madeleines,
Indulging, rich seductive dreams.

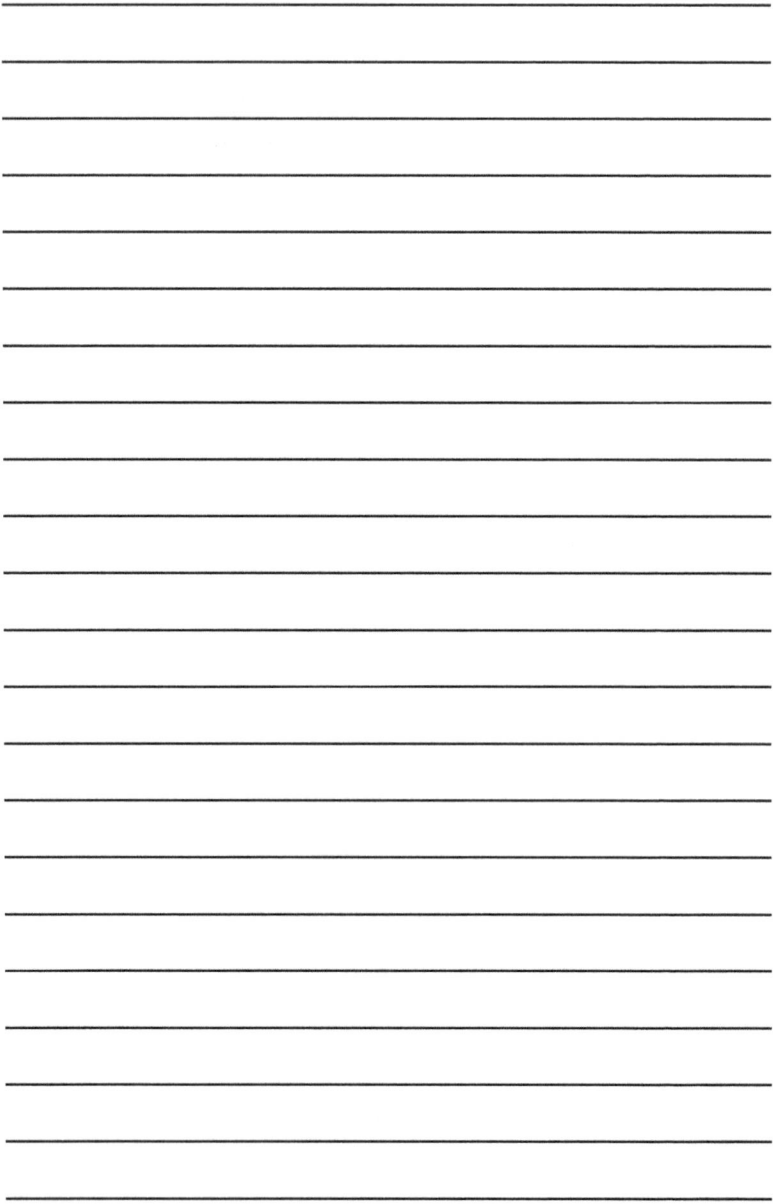

Food Truck Fling
A summer's food truck's fast delight,
Brightened kissing in back lights,
Flavorful, spontaneous bite,
Outdoor mix, culinary sight.

The Met's Masterpiece

Among maestros, my feeling shine,
Long kissing in The Met divine,
Inspired art no boundary line,
In desire's glow, cultural shrine.

__MoMA's Modern Love__
Gallery of mainstream design,
Simplicity lead art so fine,
A modern moment with a kiss,
In an collage we'd surely miss.

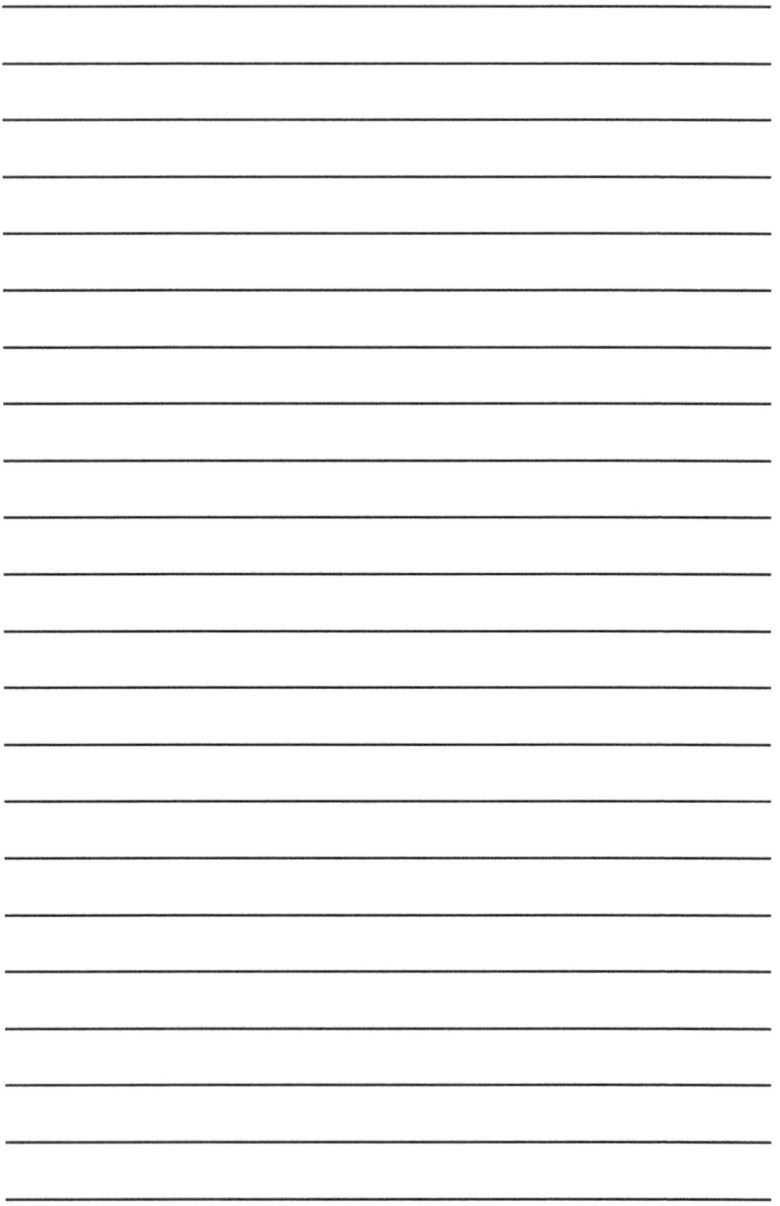

Broadway's Backstage Kiss

Behind a Broadway splendid show,
Thirsty lips wont lubricate slow,
Theater magic, hearts did seal,
In the wings wrap desire revealed.

Club Jam
Hidden in Greenwich Village lair,
Quinted rhythms guided, sweet care,
The night kissing, saxophones' sway,
Poses rulesless a jazzy way.

Graffiti City
Bushwick collective vibrant space,
New York graffiti, color face,
A quick kiss, like a mural, tells,
Urban art's beauty spray hot hails.

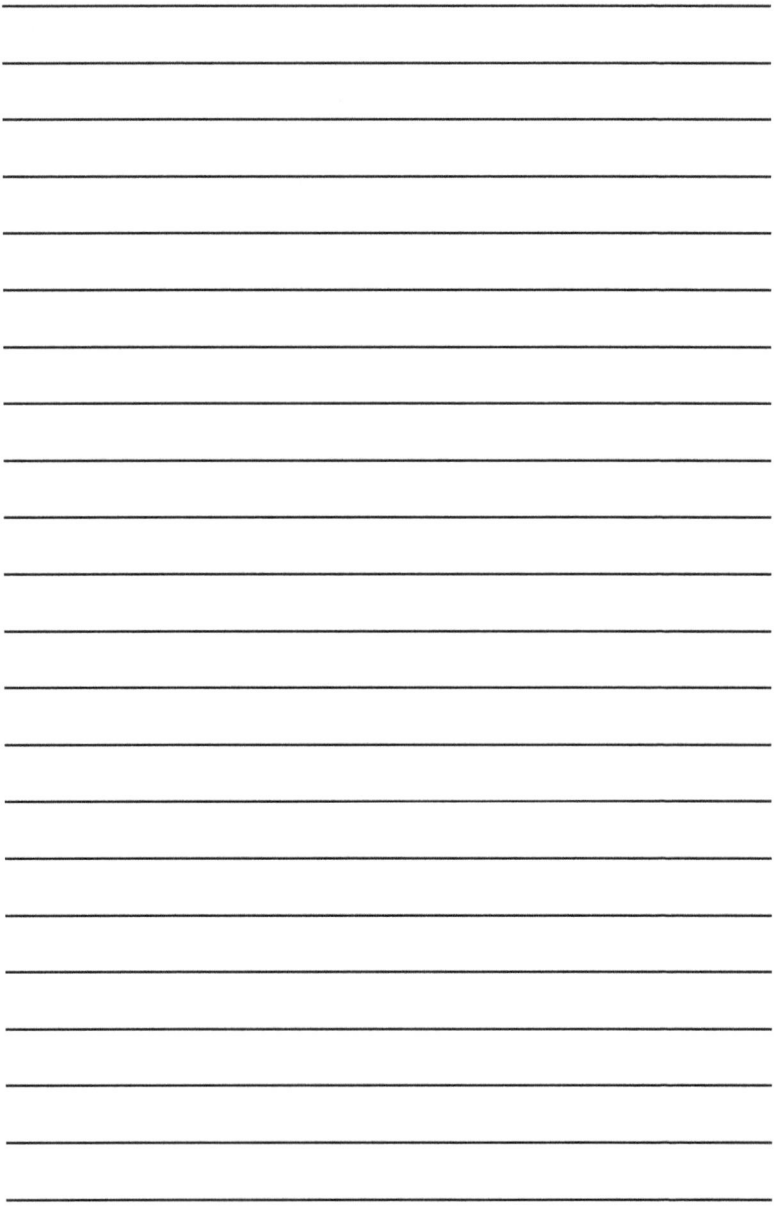

Lincoln Center's Ballet

On the lake's calm, mirror-like face,
Our gaze reflected, secret place,
A willows kiss, in rainy shoes,
Swan dance end, curtain drop, don't rush.

Central Park Lake Intimacy

Under the sun's golden light rays,
Where the clear water's gentle sway,
A kiss in the boat, moment rare,
In the lake's heart a secret shared.

_____

_____

_____

_____

_____

_____

_____

_____

_____

_____

_____

_____

_____

_____

_____

_____

_____

_____

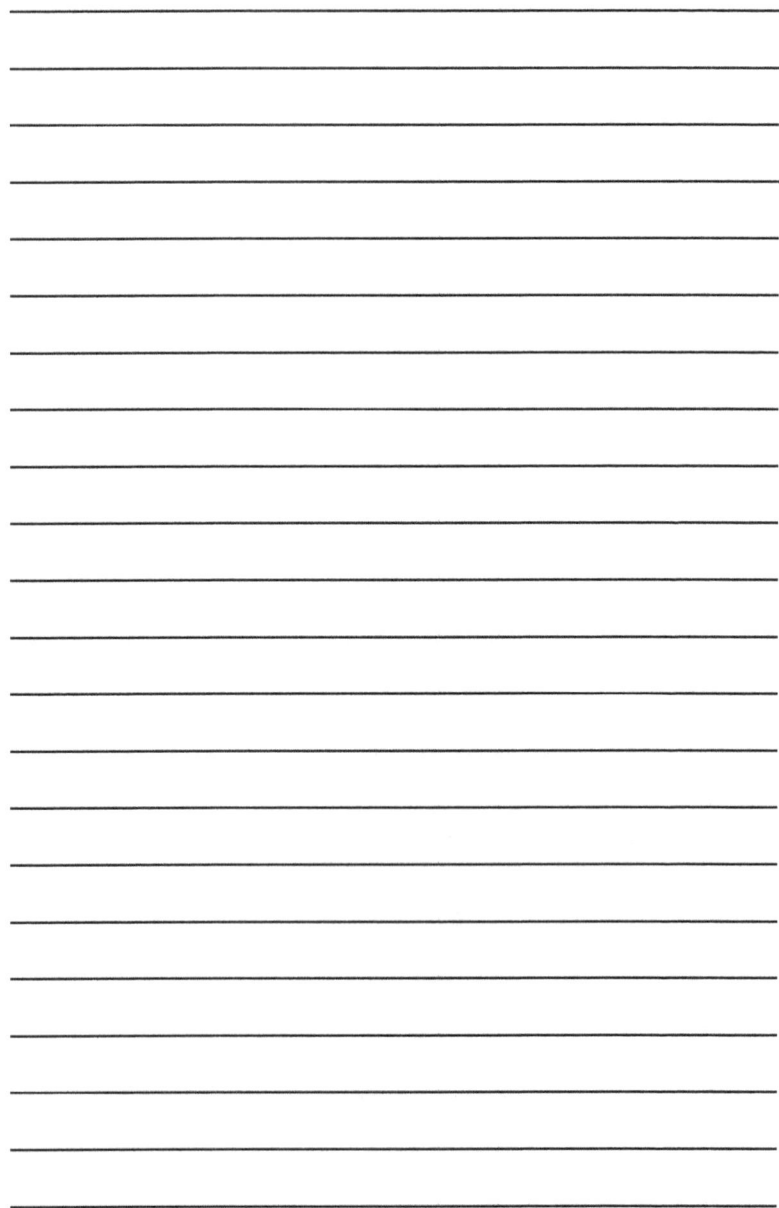

High Line Haven
Elevated above street strife,
Explore garden of urban life,
Tender lips touch, the Hudson's view,
Thrill flourished, stimulated new.

_____

_____

_____

_____

_____

_____

_____

_____

_____

_____

_____

_____

_____

_____

_____

_____

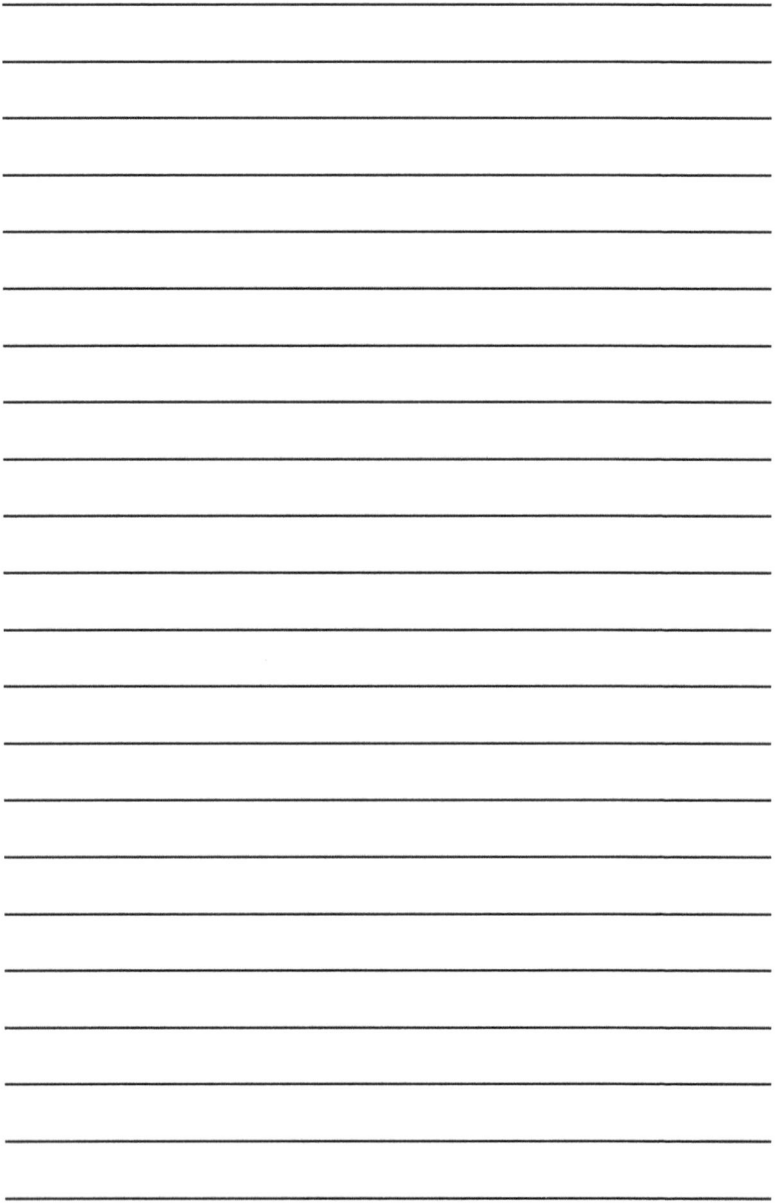

Botanic Garden Bloom

Within the roses blossoms fair,
Innocence and temptation stare,
The garden's kiss ignites a fire,
Wrapped in each other, lost desire.

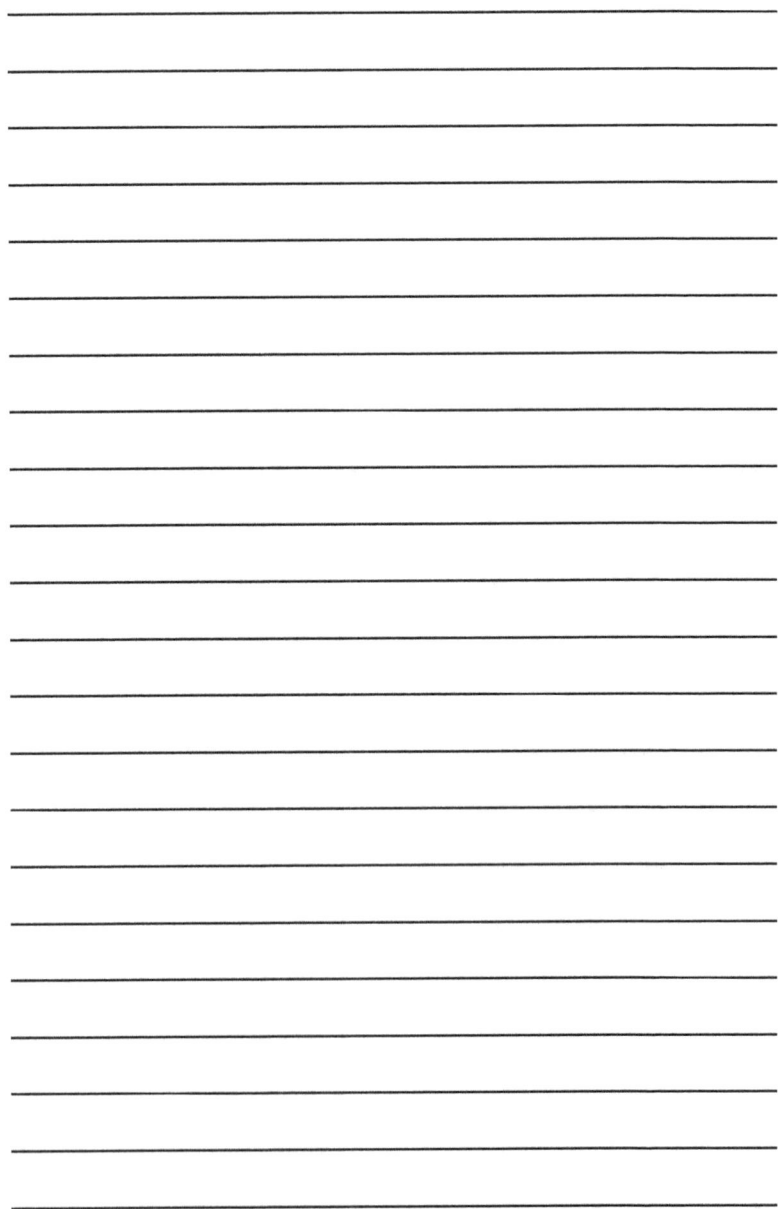

Rockaway Beach Sunset

By ocean waves where day meets night,
Our lips touch in warm, golden light,
With the surf's gentle, soothing might,
Moment shone bright in heart's soft flight.

_____

_____

_____

_____

_____

_____

_____

_____

_____

_____

_____

_____

_____

_____

_____

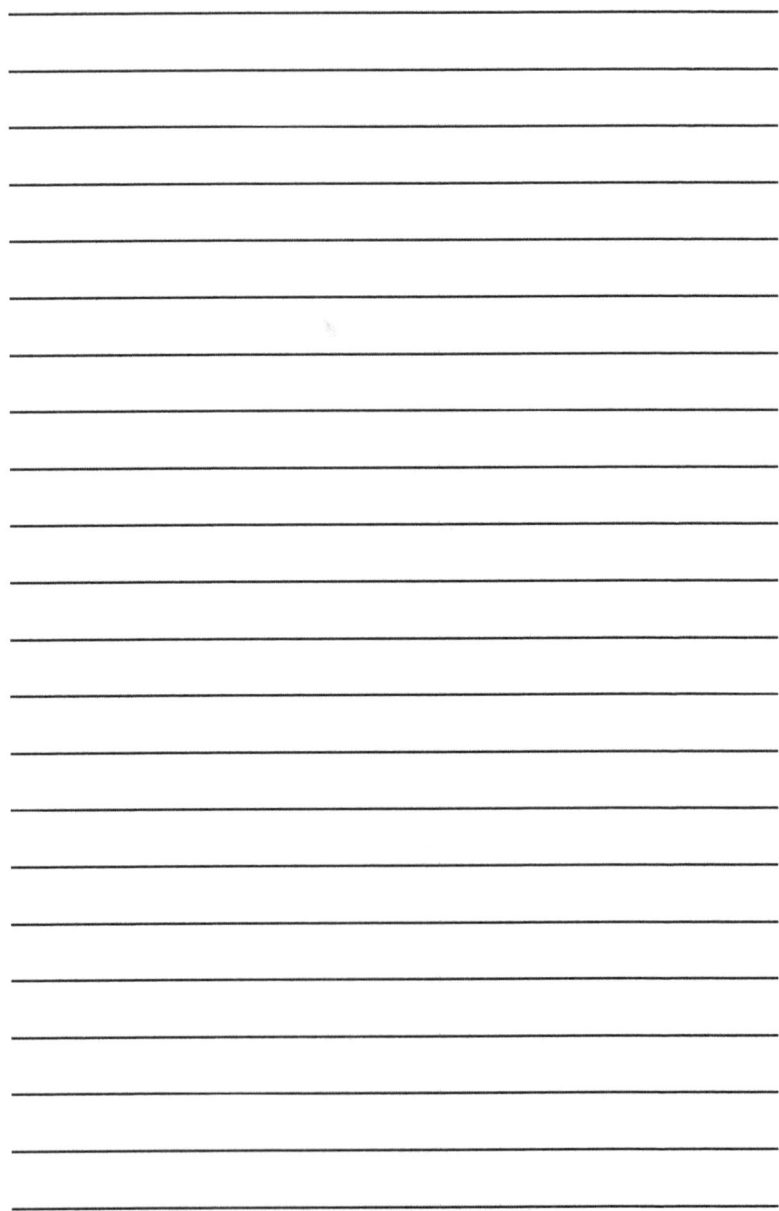

Prospect Park Picnic

Under oak trees tally and grand,
Smiles exchanged, a picnic warm land,
With each bite, a wet kiss we share,
In the park's calm air thickens fair.

The Bronx's Secret
Hidden, natural treasure rare,
Lips met lips, existence compare,
By the lake, woodland flirty view,
Lovers' promise was just renewed.

Empire Building Sparkle
A kiss beneath the city's view,
Reflecting starlight shines in you,
Manhattan's majestic sphere flight,
Closing eyes soft in nighttime light.

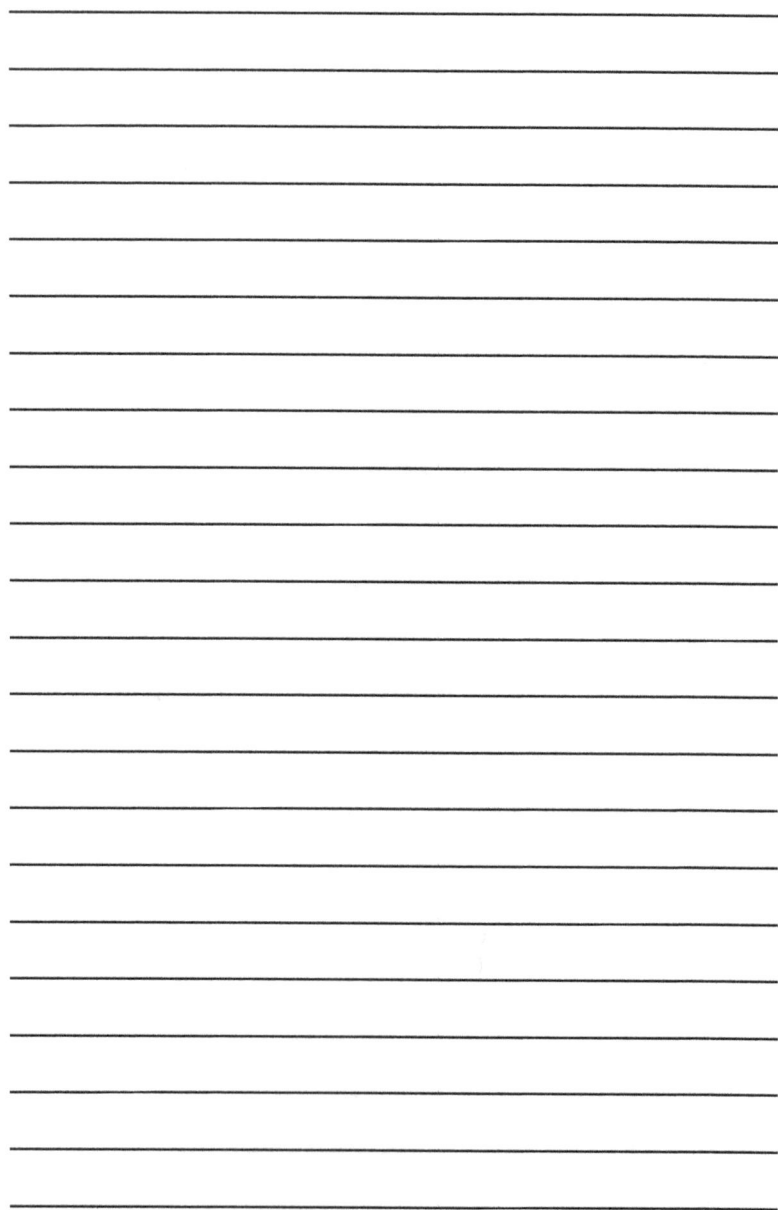

Hudson River Night Cruise
Yacht, navigates on Hudson's stream,
Champagne gleams, strawberries, weep cream,
Holding you close and kissing straight,
Through enchanting nighttime stars light.

_____

_____

_____

_____

_____

_____

_____

_____

_____

_____

_____

_____

_____

_____

_____

_____

Coney Island Fireworks

Exploding fireworks, vivid sky,
Kiss me to reach eruption high,
With every boom of blow up sound,
Coney Island's joy wonder-bound.

Greenwich Village Lanterns

Village street, lanterns cheering glow,
Strolled jointly through a peaceful flow,
Gentle kisses, jazzy notes beam,
Illuminated nighttime dream.

_____

_____

_____

_____

_____

_____

_____

_____

_____

_____

_____

_____

_____

_____

_____

_____

_____

Kiss Trade

Oculus's grand, dominant space,
Lips touched lips in sensitive grace,
The Westfield's bones reflecting light,
In perfect, nighttime kiss trade sight.

Carousel Island
Colorful carousel spins so free,
A kiss with each spin, joyful glee,
The playful, merry tune resounds,
Coney Island, fun delight found.

_____

_____

_____

_____

_____

_____

_____

_____

_____

_____

_____

_____

_____

_____

_____

_____

New York Public Library's Secret
Main reading room's in silent hush,
Whispered secrets of kissing rush,
Amidst tomes, where the wisdom found,
Don't bother us to reach the ground.

Macy's Fun
Herald Square's holiday spotlight,
Twinkling, Christmas lights fairly bright,
Spreading joyful and winter's cheer,
Passionate kisses all New Year.

_____

_____

_____

_____

_____

_____

_____

_____

_____

_____

_____

_____

_____

_____

_____

_____

_____

Carnegie Play

The Famous hall, worldwide legends roam,
Melomans hidden, tender kiss home,
Grand orchestra's gentle lead tune,
Harmonized, a Carnegie boon.

New Year's Eve
The Crystal Ball vividly descends,
Lips meet in ice glittering scene,
Midnight confetti's color display,
Times Square welcome New Year's this way.

_____

_____

_____

_____

_____

_____

_____

_____

_____

_____

_____

_____

_____

_____

_____

_____

_____

Winter Kiss

Snowflakes dance in cold moonlit glow,
Your kiss, a spark in winter's snow,
Passion's fire strike hot in your eyes,
Dreams beneath the starry clear skies.

_____

_____

_____

_____

_____

_____

_____

_____

_____

_____

_____

_____

_____

_____

_____

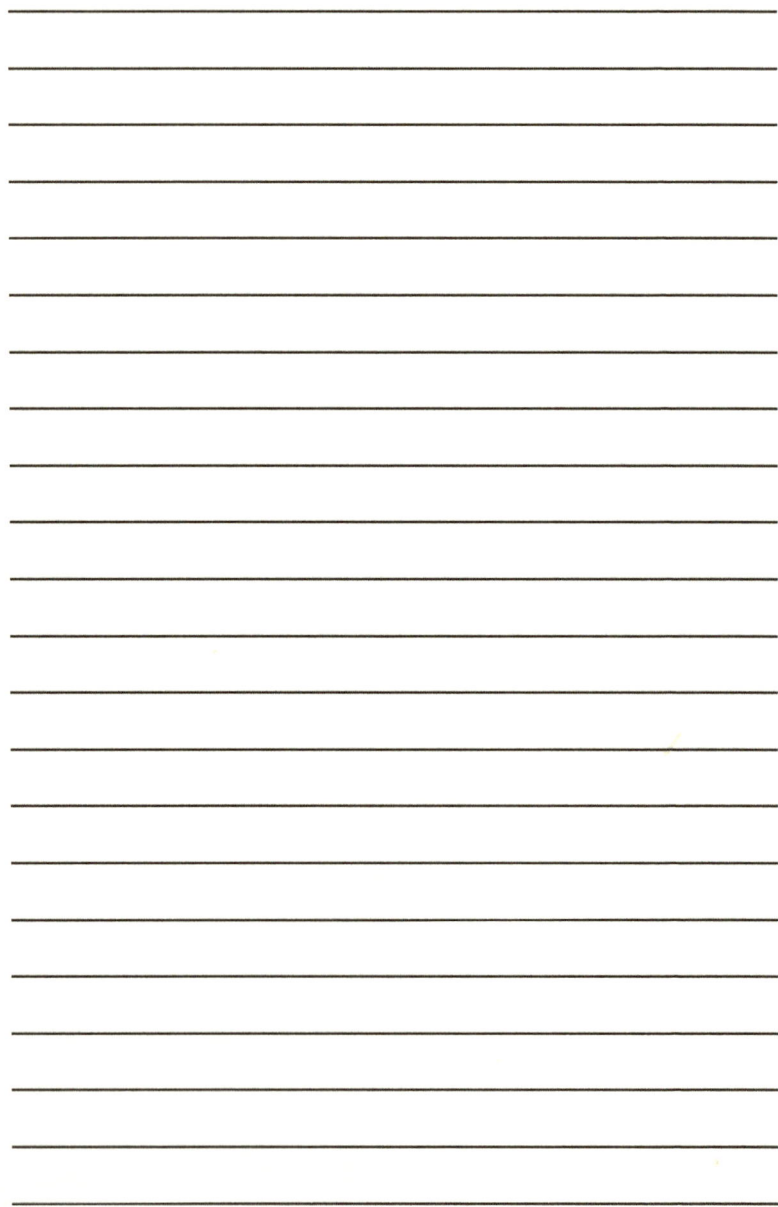

Spring Awakening
Unfolded petals dance and sway,
Prosperct Park blossom chill today,
Your gently kisses now shine bright,
Missing your hugs intensive night.

_____

_____

_____

_____

_____

_____

_____

_____

_____

_____

_____

_____

_____

_____

_____

_____

_____

Summer Love

Warm sand beneath the boardwalk's beat,
Your tongue danced in a loving treat.
Cant stop this excited movement,
Learning life's sweetest improvement.

Autumn Leaves in the Bronx
Autumn's glow fills the city's heart,
Crisp air whispers seductive start,
Golden leaves crunch soft beneath feet,
Our lips touched in autumn's warm breeze.

_____

_____

_____

_____

_____

_____

_____

_____

_____

_____

_____

_____

_____

_____

_____

_____

Valentine's Day
Candlelit plate with roses red,
Tongues entwined in shadows we're led,
Sweet and hot, in a warm embrace,
In a romantic, Village place.

_____

_____

_____

_____

_____

_____

_____

_____

_____

_____

_____

_____

_____

_____

_____

_____

_____

Halloween Celebration
West Village costumes parade flow,
Baiting your lips in spooky show,
Moonlit ecstasy time peaks burn,
Halloween scratched swingers' turns.

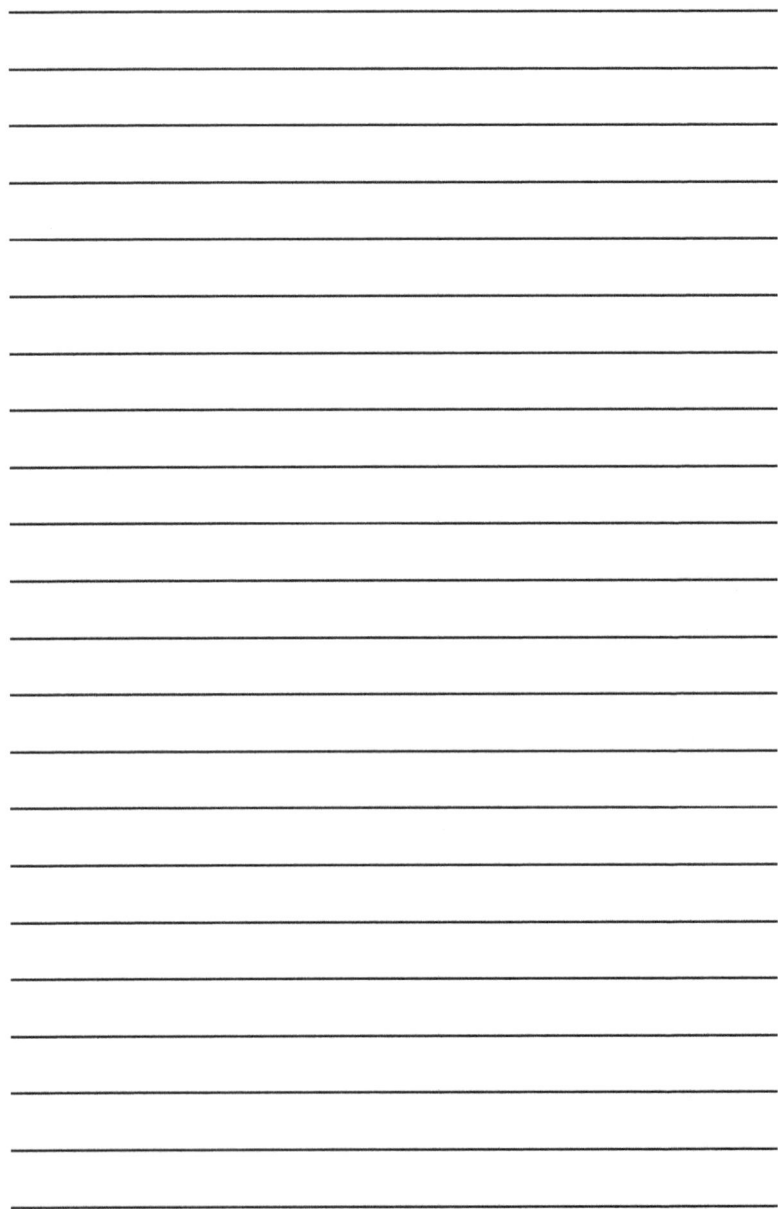

Thanksgiving Sauna
Giant balloons float thru West Side,
A festive cheer fills party tide,
Rubbing your lips, Thanksgiving Day,
Wet and throbbing, a steamy lay.

_____

_____

_____

_____

_____

_____

_____

_____

_____

_____

_____

_____

_____

_____

_____

_____

Holiday Story
Twinkling nipples, lingerie neats,
Victoria's secret hot treats,
Licking your skin on Christmas race,
Excited to reach final base.

_____

_____

_____

_____

_____

_____

_____

_____

_____

_____

_____

_____

_____

_____

_____

_____

_____

New Year's Drill
First kisses last December night,
Fireworks explode in New Year's might,
Deeper mouth penetration's thrill,
Swallow or throw, uncertain still.

_____

_____

_____

_____

_____

_____

_____

_____

_____

_____

_____

_____

_____

_____

_____

_____

_____

Rockefeller Eggs
Last ice melts, Rockefeller's prime,
Tulips spread petals, sex design,
As Easter bunny, I'm between,
Spring's lures, "Come-on", nurse jelly bin.

Coney Island Warm

The Cyclone's thrilling roar choking,
Sunny beach wet lips provoking,
You cover summer's woody stand,
But need more legs now than your hand

_____

_____

_____

_____

_____

_____

_____

_____

_____

_____

_____

_____

_____

_____

_____

_____

_____

The Little Red Lighthouse's Charm
Beneath the bridge, a secret glow,
A lighthouse stands where passions flow.
Your lips on mine, a fiery kiss,
In shadows deep, desire's abyss.

_____

_____

_____

_____

_____

_____

_____

_____

_____

_____

_____

_____

_____

_____

_____

_____

_____

No *Intimacy* Room

Gentlemen's den, where beauties sway,
Sensual lap dance performers way.
Try taste your lips, its forbidden thrill,
But club rules dictate, must stand still.

_____

_____

_____

_____

_____

_____

_____

_____

_____

_____

_____

_____

_____

_____

_____

_____

Historic Brownstones Journey
Tree-lined streets, elegant brownstones,
Picturesque, floating pheromones,
Nobody looking, dusky land,
Hook kissing. In A T M stand.

The Brooklyn Lyceum's
New cultural, artistic tree
Possessing your topless selfie
Running to kiss you on our break,
Piano, bed, table, chair, strike.

Top of The Rock

Let's elevate up next daydream,
Your glossy lips ready to beam,
Valentine heart shines on facade,
Celebrating first kiss decade.

Rossy Bath

Heart longs for a rose-petal soak.
Greeting with champagne's provoke,
Tender kiss to welcome the night,
Drink bubbles from the kitty's hide.

Hudson Park Intimacy
Iconic scenes at vibrant sight,
Classic tango invites tonight
Sensual kisses find perfect pair,
Hudson Park's promenade affair.

Manhattan
Whiskey, sweet vermouth and bitters,
Pink skyline, moment for cheaters,
Naked body erotic scent,
Kissing neck, hard nipples, extend.

A Central Park's Game
Park's gardens strip, a King's could might,
Meets a Queen, beauty rare in sight,
Lips touch on a board desire quest,
Bishop, Rock or Pawn be next guest.

Yellow Taxi Night Ride
The doors slammed shut, the car took off,
In each other's arms like before,
Come back to me, tonight, I miss
Our crazy life and every kiss.

Chelsea Pier Bar
Searching for you, drinking alone,
Maybe you're here, club leading tone,
Crowds enjoy the scene, red dress near,
Kissing chilly lips, stay here dear.

Whispers in the New York Public Library
Among the shelves of ancient tomes,
Our reverent, loving syndromes,
Kiss you gently, stroking wet slit,
Somebody walked in, take a hit.

_____

_____

_____

_____

_____

_____

_____

_____

_____

_____

_____

_____

_____

_____

_____

_____

_____

Enchanted Evening at the Plaza Hotel
Chandeliers, enjoy the tea,
Special day, will you marry me?
Yes! Long kiss, hug, glasses breake, smile,
Plaza Hotel, lovely rich style.

_____

_____

_____

_____

_____

_____

_____

_____

_____

_____

_____

_____

_____

_____

_____

_____

_____

_____

Brooklyn Bridge's Bathroom.
Enter behind your shower heat,
Golden rain are kissing your feet,
Hold round breasts, my body nearer.
Together ending... Steamed mirror.

East Village Cinema

Empty room with your flashing eyes,
Bare foot check in if I'm ready.
Unzip, massage, swallow. My part:
Tongue, fingers, whole hand… Movie start.

Long time no see
Play with four pearls, you and your friend
Only two hands, testing chests scent,
Wine break, double ride, flip and blend
Great end of date former students.

Closed Chelsea Bar
Hundreds bras hangs above the bar,
Tube challenges guests take off your scar,
Hot lips kiss wine, served directly,
Hunting lingerie erectly.

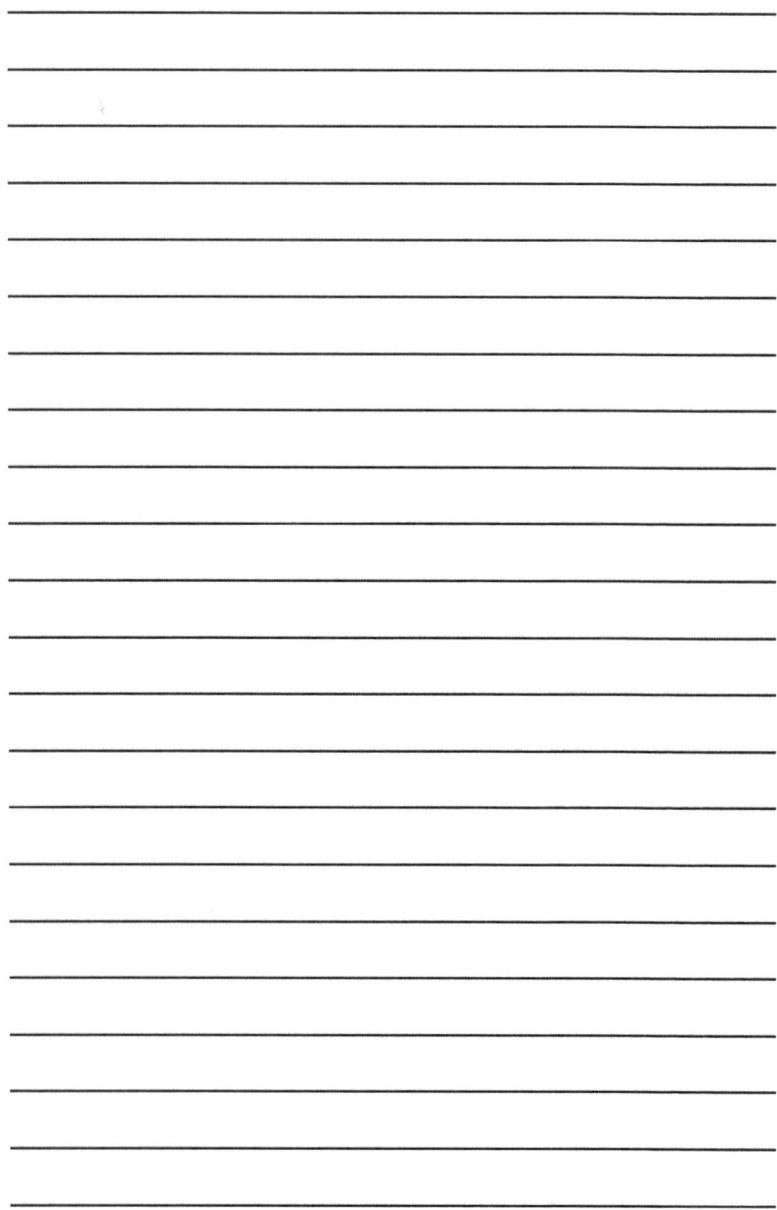

New Year in Chinatown
Burgundy nails ripping my lips,
Snake dance, excited to bite hips,
Torn crop, confetti rocketeer,
Scratched back, neck, Happy New Year!

_____

_____

_____

_____

_____

_____

_____

_____

_____

_____

_____

_____

_____

_____

_____

_____

_____

Guggenheim Spiral Kiss Design
Narrow toilets golden granit,
Body against body, bare fit,
Scent of nude fabric, dress strap falls.
Tempting attraction of linked lips.

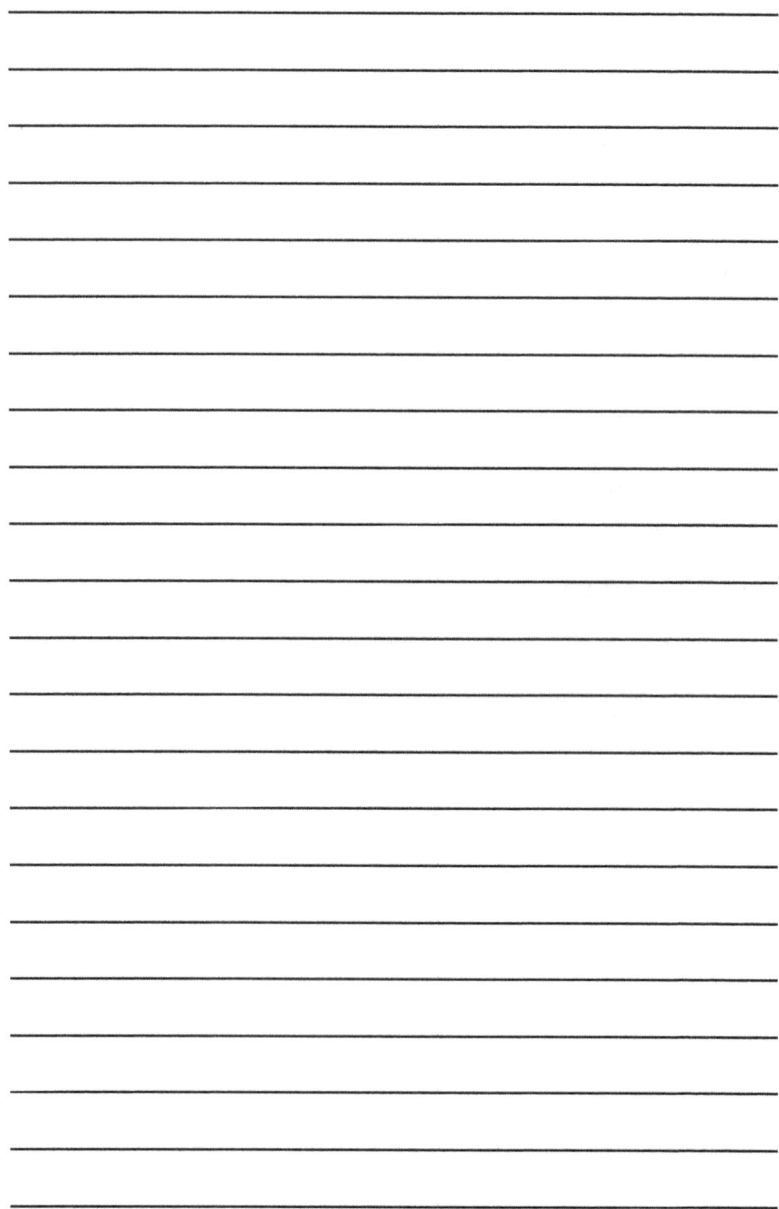

City View
Stormy weather, scattered nylons,
Half-drunk champagne, flowers swans,
By the window, we kiss naked,
United, our warmth forsaken.

_____

_____

_____

_____

_____

_____

_____

_____

_____

_____

_____

_____

_____

_____

_____

Rooftop Garden
Naked people in the spa wash,
White gloves staff, pleasure massage
By four hands, savoring the taste
More tongues, I want everywhere traced.

Grand Central Terminal's Whispering Kiss

Farewell's brief moment, may it stay
And in memory, never stray,
My lips on yours, a tender bite,
Savoring taste, of our last night.

A Broadway Limousine Route

Midtown bars - Chinatown hotel,
Limousine, caught traffic is well.
Legs spread wide, waiting for quickie,
A taste of night, moist and sticky.

_____

_____

_____

_____

_____

_____

_____

_____

_____

_____

_____

_____

_____

_____

_____

_____

_____

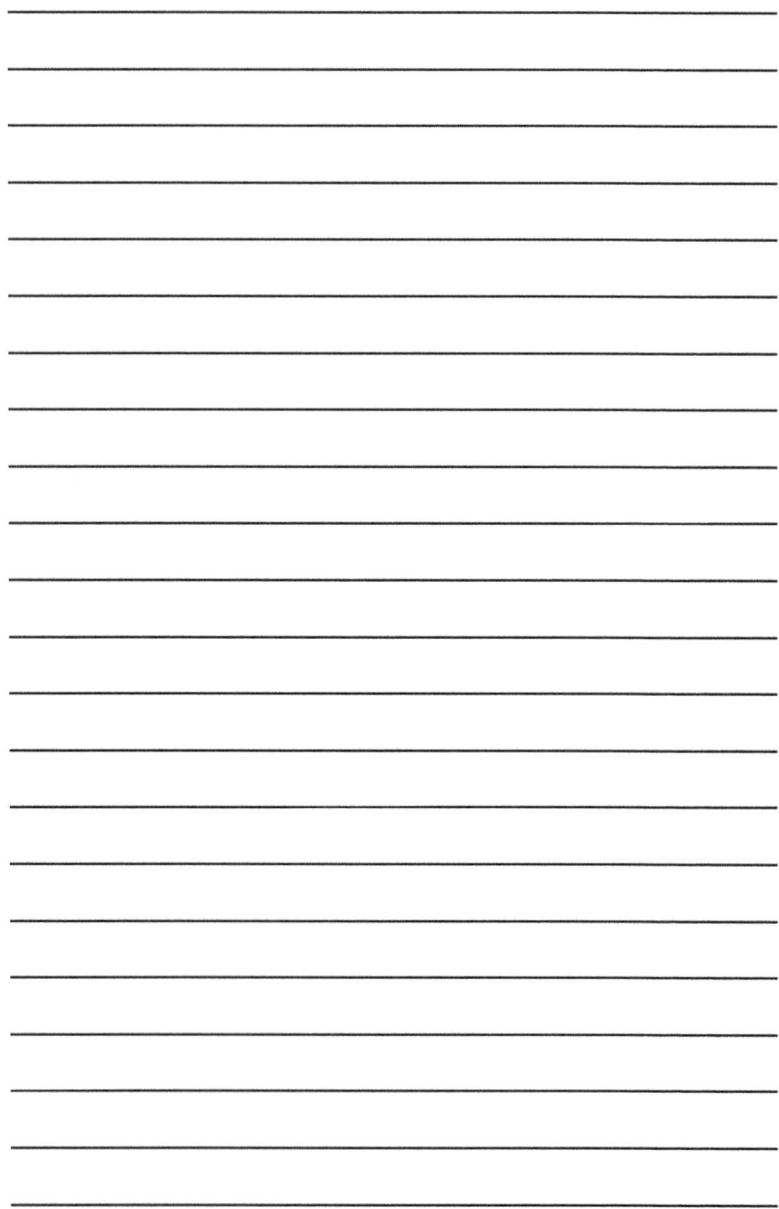

Photographing You

Each shot undress you, remove shame,
Kiss your body before each frame,
Discover spread hair, open drums
Wild soft mouth, goosebumps, womb comes.

_____

_____

_____

_____

_____

_____

_____

_____

_____

_____

_____

_____

_____

_____

_____

_____

_____

Tempest

Anger's fierce scream glass shatters floor,
Heavy ashtray crashes once more,
Night's envelop me, kiss impart,
Fury spent, smile reaches my heart.